Be a Vessel of Honor

Allowing God's Glory to Shape Your Life

by Gloria Copeland

JESUS IS LORD

KENNETH
COPELAND
PUBLICATIONS

Unless otherwise noted, all scripture is from the *King James Version* of the Bible.

Scripture quotations marked *The Amplified Bible* are from *The Amplified Bible, Old Testament* © 1965, 1987 by The Zondervan Corporation. *The Amplified New Testament* © 1958, 1987 by The Lockman Foundation. Used by permission.

Scripture quotations marked *New International Version* are from *The Holy Bible, New International Version* ®, © 1973, 1978, 1984 by the International Bible Society. Used by permission of Zondervan Publishing House.

Be a Vessel of Honor,
Allowing God's Glory to Shape Your Life

ISBN 1-57562-714-0   30-0551

08 07 06 05 04 03   7 6 5 4 3 2

Kenneth Copeland Ministries
Fort Worth, Texas 76192-0001

For more information about Kenneth Copeland Ministries, call 1-800-600-7395 or visit www.kcm.org

Be a Vessel of Honor
Allowing God's Glory
to Shape Your Life

You and I live in an amazing time. It is a time of great spiritual light...and a time of great spiritual darkness.

Today Christians have more revelation of the Word of God than any other generation that has ever lived. Yet the world around us is growing more evil every day. Evidence of it is everywhere. If you turn on the evening news, you'll hear one report after another of awful things people have done to one another—and sometimes it's what they have done to one of their own family members.

It seems that people today even applaud evil. If you flip through the TV channels, you're sure to come across a talk show—and you have to wonder where they find people who talk about the things they do! These talk shows cover all kinds of depraved topics. And when they get the most depraved, that's when the audience claps the most!

What Are We to Do?

How are we as believers supposed to live in the midst of such evil? God's instructions are very clear: *"Abstain from evil [shrink from it and keep aloof from it] in whatever form or whatever kind it may be"* (1 Thessalonians 5:22, *The Amplified Bible*).

Abstain from evil. That means don't participate in it, don't watch it, don't feed on it, have nothing to do with it. As born-again believers, we are not children of the dark. We are children of the light. We've been translated out of the kingdom of darkness and into the kingdom of God's dear Son

(Colossians 1:13). We have no business participating in evil. We have to turn entirely away from it.

First Thessalonians 5 goes on to say:

And may the God of peace Himself sanctify you through and through [separate you from profane things, make you pure and wholly consecrated to God]; and may your spirit and soul and body be preserved sound and complete [and found] blameless at the coming of our Lord Jesus Christ (the Messiah). Faithful is He Who is calling you [to Himself] and utterly trustworthy, and He will also do it [fulfill His call by hallowing and keeping you] (verses 23-24, *The Amplified Bible*).

You and I are to be devoted to the Lord. He is calling us to Himself. He is calling us to be separated from evil and profane things, and to be consecrated and *devoted* to Him.

Devoted to God...or Destruction?

God wants us to be holy—and 1 Corinthians 3:16-17 says it this way, "*Know* ye not that ye are the temple of God, and that the Spirit of God dwelleth in you? If any man defile [or destroy] the temple of God, him shall God destroy; for the temple of God is holy."

The "temple" in this scripture is your body. And according to this verse, our bodies are to be holy.

To be holy means to be set apart, to be separated *unto* something and separated *from* something else. Recently, as I was thinking about that, I was reminded of something else in the Word that God calls holy—the tithe. Suddenly, I realized that our bodies are much like the tithe!

The Bible teaches us that the tithe is *devoted* (just like God wants us to be). That means it has been set aside for God. It's a holy thing. It's set apart for God's use. If you're a believer and in covenant with God, every time you increase, 10 percent of that increase is holy. If you don't tithe, that 10 percent still belongs to God and the Bible says you are robbing God.

The Hebrew word in Scripture that means devoted, *charman*, actually means "devoted to destruction." So a person's tithe can be devoted to God or to destruction. If they give it to God, it becomes devoted to Him. If they keep it, and rob Him of it, it becomes devoted to destruction.

Now, in the light of that, let's read 1 Corinthians 3:16-17 again: *"Know ye not that ye are the temple of God, and that the Spirit of God dwelleth in you? If any man defile* [or destroy] *the temple of God, him shall God destroy; for the temple of God is holy."*

Just like the tithe, your body, the temple of the Holy Spirit, is holy. And just like if you withhold the tithe it will be devoted to destruction, if you defile your body it will be on a course for destruction as well.

If you don't keep your body the way you should, by obeying God, your body will begin to destruct. This is the law of sowing and reaping in action. The more a person takes drugs, drinks alcohol, partakes in pornography or adultery, and all other kinds of sin, the more quickly he or she will die.

Can this be true for a believer? Yes. The law of sowing and reaping works just like natural laws that govern this earth. Gravity works for believers and unbelievers alike. So does the law of sowing and reaping.

Let's take this a step further. Consider this in regard to your body and healing. Your body is holy, set apart, consecrated, devoted. Therefore, no sickness or disease has a right in your body. No sickness or disease has a right in the temple of God—and that temple has no business living in an unholy or carnal way.

God has called us, as His sons and daughters, to live set apart and sanctified... holy. To be holy simply means that we obey God in everything He tells us to do—that we live for Him and stop participating in the world's ways.

God Wants You Free

I believe every believer who loves God wants to be holy. But not every believer is actually living holy. Many times we have old habits we've never overcome, even though we've lived with them for years.

If you've struggled like this, even for years, I know you can be free. God wants you free, and the Scripture says the truth will make you free. If you continue in the Word of God, it will make you free and you can live holy.

Jesus said in His prayer to the Father, *"Sanctify them through thy truth: thy word is truth"* (John 17:17). I don't care if what's holding you back is the strongest addiction there is, God will set you free. All He needs is your choice, your quality decision that,

9

"No matter what, this is it. I'm leaving bondage behind."

God is faithful. He's just waiting on the opportunity to help you. He is a merciful and loving Father. Jeremiah 15:19 says, *"Therefore thus saith the Lord, If thou return, then will I bring thee again, and thou shalt stand before me: and if thou take forth the precious from the vile, thou shalt be as my mouth: let them return unto thee; but return not thou unto them."*

"If thou return...." As a believer, that's what God's asking you to do—to draw nigh unto Him and He'll draw nigh unto you with every deliverance, every blessing, every prosperity that you need. If you're a person who's moved away from God, He's asking you to return. If you've never been saved, He's asking you to come to Him and make Jesus your Lord and Savior.

"The precious from the vile...." He wants us to learn to separate in our lives the precious things that are His from the vile things of

this world. God won't force you to do that. He doesn't require you to live a life separated unto Him because He wants to be a dictator. No. That's not God's way at all.

God wants you to do what He says and walk in His ways because they produce freedom. They produce the best for you. You can't walk in the ways of the world and be free. God loves you. He wants you to be able to wake up every morning happy, full of joy, with your needs met, your family around you, and no trouble on any side. And He wants you to be free of all those things you've struggled with for years.

He's Never Stopped Working

You may have given up on overcoming some things in your life, but God never has. You may have thought it was just impossible, that you'd just have to live with it, whatever it may be. But God has never thought that way. His word to you is ALL THINGS ARE POSSIBLE!

For example, as I was reading some scriptures about being perfect, which means to come into maturity, I found that *The Amplified Bible* included in the meaning to be restored or readjusted.

From the time you came into the kingdom of God, God has endeavored to restore you, to readjust you so that you can walk in the full blessings and the full power of God. He's desired for you to walk holy and unhindered.

Jeremiah 18:1-4 says:

The word which came to Jeremiah from the Lord: Arise and go down to the potter's house, and there I will cause you to hear My words. Then I went down to the potter's house, and behold, he was working at the wheel. And the vessel that he was making from clay was spoiled in the hand of the potter; so he made it over, reworking it into another vessel as it seemed good to the potter to make it *(The Amplified Bible)*.

When Ken and I celebrated our 30th year in the ministry in 1997, we did a lot of reminiscing. We recounted many things that had transpired over the years. And we remembered mistakes we had made.

But God just kept working and kept readjusting and restoring and giving us more revelation, so that we could live and think a little higher as we kept going. More than thirty years have come and gone, and He's never left the potter's wheel. He's still working, still forming, still teaching, still training us to live for Him...free from everything that could hold us back from more of Him.

God's doing the same thing for you. He didn't quit on Ken and me, and He won't quit on you. You may be at your lowest point ever. You may be thinking you're never going to do anything of worth in this life. But God has a plan for you. *"For I know the plans*

I have for you,' declares the Lord, 'plans to prosper you and not to harm you, plans to give you hope and a future'" (Jeremiah 29:11, *New International Version*).

Brother Kenneth Hagin prophesied to Ken more than 20 years ago about things that are just now happening in our ministry. God's had it all under control. He knew how to get us out of situations, mature us and get us to this place where we are now. And He knows how to get you out of the situation you're in and get you to where He wants you to be. He knows how to get you to a higher level. He knows how to get you free, if you'll just continue in His Word.

That's all you and I have to do, and we can always do our part. God can always do the impossible part. God and sons—what an awesome team!

You Are an Earthen Vessel

No matter what you do in life, or where you go, God is on top of the situation. Because He loves you, He's committed to helping you change.

Second Corinthians 3:17-18 says:

Now the Lord is that Spirit: and where the Spirit of the Lord is, there is liberty. But we all, with open face beholding as in a glass the glory of the Lord, are changed into the same image from glory to glory, even as by the Spirit of the Lord.

We are being changed into the image of God, from glory to glory. We weren't born again one day and suddenly full-grown Christians the next. We had to grow and grow, little by little. And we grew by the Word of God.

The scripture in 2 Corinthians 4:6-7 says:

For God, who commanded the light to shine out of darkness, hath shined in our hearts, to give the light of the knowledge of the glory of God in the face of Jesus Christ. But we have this treasure in earthen vessels, that the excellency of the power may be of God, and not of us.

The treasure in the earthen vessels is the glory of God. And an earthen vessel is a temple of the Holy Spirit—or your body! It's the temple that God said must be sanctified and set apart for Him. It's a temple devoted to God—a holy thing.

We cannot walk in the full blessing of God without living a sanctified life. God has a work to do in these last days, and He will have a people who are dedicated to Him. He's going to have vessels full of His glory— the glory that He wants to manifest in these last days.

Hath not the potter power over the clay, of the same lump to make one vessel unto honour, and another unto dishonour? What if God, willing to show his wrath, and to make his power known, endured with much long-suffering the vessels of wrath fitted to destruction: And that he might make known the riches of his glory on the vessels of mercy, which he had afore prepared unto glory (Romans 9:21-23).

God has been preparing vessels—vessels of mercy and glory. Just like the tithe and your body, which can be devoted to destruction or devoted to the Lord, there are two kinds of human vessels in the earth. There are vessels of wrath—fitted for destruction, and vessels of mercy—fitted for glory.

The vessels fitted for destruction are people who think they've been getting away with the things they've done, but they really haven't gotten away with anything. God has simply endured their sin with long-suffering, giving them opportunity to come to Him.

The vessels of mercy are believers who have been prepared to receive God's end-time manifestations of the glory. We are being set apart. We are the temples of the Holy Spirit. We are the ones who are to keep our bodies separated unto God and away from profane and unholy things. We're to be vessels fitted for glory.

You Can Be a Vessel of Honor

As we desire to be vessels fitted for glory, and to live holy, we have to make choices. God will help us...but we have our part to do. Second Timothy 2:15-17, 20-21 instructs us to:

> Study to show thyself approved unto God, a workman that needeth not to be ashamed, rightly dividing the word of truth. But shun profane and vain babblings: for they will increase unto more ungodliness. And their word will eat as doth a canker....But in a great house there are not only vessels of gold and of silver, but also of wood and of earth; and some to honour, and some to dishonour. If a man therefore purge himself from these, he shall be a vessel unto honour, sanctified, and meet for the master's use, and prepared unto every good work.

How is it determined whether we will be vessels of honor or vessels of dishonor? Does God say, "I'm going to make this one a vessel of honor, and since this one doesn't count for squat, I'm going to make him a vessel of dishonor"?

No, not at all! *"If a man therefore purge himself...."*

"If a man...." You do it, and I do it. We decide what kind of vessels we'll be...ones of dishonor, fitted for destruction, or ones of honor, fitted for glory.

God leaves the choice up to us. He's asking us to purge ourselves from the things that are not right in His sight. He wants us to be free and holy, so we can be vessels of honor.

He has miracles to perform through His vessels. He has signs and wonders He wants to manifest. He has some outstanding work planned for us. He intends to gather to Himself all of the people in the earth who will come to Him.

He is not a God of wrath. He is a God of justice. He's like the potter, ever working, ever adjusting to lead us on a path of righteousness, a path filled with good, a path filled with benefits.

Find out what the Word of God says about holiness. Find out what it says about being vessels of honor and dishonor. Begin to do what the Word says. When you do, it will be harder for the evil of the world to stick to you.

Don't focus anymore on what you've struggled with for years. Don't focus on what all you can't do. Focus on what you can do— you can spend time in the Word. And as you do, the Word will separate you from the things of this world, the addictions you've been fighting, the sin with which you've struggled.

If you stay with the Word, sooner or later those things will fall away. Those habits will disappear. You just keep following righteousness. You keep going after God's Word and walking in faith. You keep walking in love and following peace. Fellowship with people who call upon the Lord out of a pure heart, and the first thing you know, those old trappings will be nowhere in sight.

They won't be in your spirit, your body or your mind. You won't want drugs and alcohol anymore. You won't want a cigarette anymore. You won't want immorality in your life anymore.

Make your choice today: "I'm going for God. I'm ridding myself of this junk that has been hanging on me. I'm going after freedom. I'm choosing to be a vessel fitted for glory."

I believe you're willing. I believe you want to be holy. I believe you want to be a temple devoted to the Lord. I believe you are the temple of God! Pray this with me...

Father, I love Your Word and I take it into my heart. In Jesus' Name I purge myself of everything displeasing to You. I choose right now to be free and to make a change, to go for more of You. I choose not to hold back or to draw back because I know that gives You no pleasure. I walk by faith and step on out, Lord. I step out on the water, to walk on the water with You, to put aside everything that is displeasing to You.

I want to be a vessel fitted, ready, filled, useful, for the glory of God. I want the glory of God to be manifest through the Church in this day to the degree that You desire. I humble myself under Your mighty hand. I prefer others and walk in love.

I make myself available to You. I want to be fit and ready for any good work. I don't care who You move through, Lord, but I want You to move. I want You to have full freedom so I offer myself unto You to be fully obedient, sanctified and set apart. My body is the temple of the Holy Ghost. I yield myself to your Holy Spirit, I set myself to renew my mind in line with Your Word. I give You all the praise and all the glory in Jesus' Name. Amen.

Prayer for Salvation and Baptism in the Holy Spirit

Heavenly Father, I come to You in the Name of Jesus. Your Word says, "Whosoever shall call on the name of the Lord shall be saved" (Acts 2:21). I am calling on You. I pray and ask Jesus to come into my heart and be Lord over my life according to Romans 10:9-10. "If thou shalt confess with thy mouth the Lord Jesus, and shalt believe in thine heart that God hath raised him from the dead, thou shalt be saved. For with the heart man believeth unto righteousness; and with the mouth confession is made unto salvation." I do that now. I confess that Jesus is Lord, and I believe in my heart that God raised Him from the dead.

I am now reborn! I am a Christian—a child of Almighty God! I am saved! You also said in Your Word, "If ye then, being evil, know how to give good gifts unto your children: HOW MUCH MORE shall your heavenly Father give the Holy Spirit to them that ask him?" (Luke 11:13). I'm also asking You to fill me with the Holy Spirit. Holy Spirit, rise up within me as I praise God. I fully expect to speak with other tongues as You give me the utterance (Acts 2:4). In Jesus' Name. Amen!

Begin to praise God for filling you with the Holy Spirit. Speak those words and syllables you receive—not in your own language, but the language given to you by the Holy Spirit. You have to use your own voice. God will not force you to speak. Don't be concerned with how it sounds. It is a heavenly language!

Continue with the blessing God has given you and pray in the spirit every day.

You are a born-again, Spirit-filled believer. You'll never be the same!

Find a good church that boldy preaches God's Word and obeys it. Become a part of a church family who will love and care for you as you love and care for them.

We need to be connected to each other. It increases our strength in God. It's God's plan for us.

Make it a habit to watch the *Believer's Voice of Victory* television broadcast and become a doer of the Word, who is blessed in his doing (James 1:22-25).

About the Author

Gloria Copeland is an author and minister of the gospel whose teaching ministry is known throughout the world. Believers worldwide know her through Believers' Conventions, Victory Campaigns, magazine articles, teaching tapes and videos, and the daily and Sunday Believer's Voice of Victory television broadcast, which she hosts with her husband, Kenneth Copeland. She is known for "Healing School," which she began teaching and hosting in 1979 at KCM meetings. Gloria delivers the Word of God and the keys to victorious Christian living to millions of people every year.

Gloria has written many books, including God's Will for You, Walk With God, God's Will Is Prosperity, Hidden Treasures and Are You Listening? She has also co-authored several books with her husband, including Family Promises, Healing Promises and the best-selling daily devotional, Pursuit of His Presence.

She holds an honorary doctorate from Oral Roberts University. In 1994, Gloria was voted Christian Woman of the Year, an honor conferred on women whose example demonstrates outstanding Christian leadership. Gloria is also the co-founder and vice-president of Kenneth Copeland Ministries in Fort Worth, Texas.

Learn more about
Kenneth Copeland Ministries
by visiting our Web site at **www.kcm.org**

Materials to Help You Receive Your Healing

by Gloria Copeland

Books

* And Jesus Healed Them All

  God's Prescription for Divine Health

* Harvest of Health

Audiotapes

God Is a Good God

God Wants You Well

Healing School

Videotapes

Healing School: God Wants You Well

Know Him as Healer

Books Available From Kenneth Copeland Ministries

by Kenneth Copeland

* A Ceremony of Marriage
  A Matter of Choice
  Covenant of Blood
  Faith and Patience—The Power Twins
* Freedom From Fear
  Giving and Receiving
  Honor—Walking in Honesty, Truth and Integrity
  How to Conquer Strife
  How to Discipline Your Flesh
  How to Receive Communion
  Know Your Enemy
  Living at the End of Time—A Time of Supernatural Increase
  Living the Laws of Prosperity and the Life God Blesses
  Love Never Fails
* Mercy—The Divine Rescue of the Human Race
* Now Are We in Christ Jesus
* Our Covenant With God
  Partnership, Sharing the Vision—Sharing the Grace
* Prayer—Your Foundation for a Life of Success
* Prosperity: The Choice Is Yours
  Rumors of War
* Sensitivity of Heart
* Six Steps to Excellence in Ministry
* Sorrow Not! Winning Over Grief and Sorrow
* The Decision Is Yours
* The Force of Faith

by Gloria Copeland

* Love—The Secret to Your Success
  No Deposit—No Return
  Pleasing the Father
  Pressing In—It's Worth It All
  Shine On!
  The Grace That Makes Us Holy
  The Power to Live a New Life
  The Unbeatable Spirit of Faith
* Walk in the Spirit (Available in Spanish only)
  Walk With God
  Well Worth the Wait
  Your Promise of Protection—The Power of the 91st Psalm

Books Co-Authored by Kenneth and Gloria Copeland

Family Promises
Healing Promises
Prosperity Promises
Protection Promises

* From Faith to Faith—A Daily Guide to Victory
  From Faith to Faith—A Perpetual Calendar

One Word From God Series
• One Word From God Can Change Your Destiny
• One Word From God Can Change Your Family
• One Word From God Can Change Your Finances
• One Word From God Can Change Your Formula
  for Success
• One Word From God Can Change Your Health
• One Word From God Can Change Your Nation

- One Word From God Can Change Your Prayer Life
- One Word From God Can Change Your Relationships

Over The Edge—A Youth Devotional
Load Up—A Youth Devotional
Pursuit of His Presence—A Daily Devotional
Pursuit of His Presence—A Perpetual Calendar

Other Books Published by KCP

The First 30 Years—A Journey of Faith
  The story of the lives of Kenneth and Gloria Copeland.
Real People. Real Needs. Real Victories.
  A book of testimonies to encourage your faith.
John G. Lake—His Life, His Sermons, His Boldness of Faith
The Holiest of All by Andrew Murray
The New Testament in Modern Speech
  by Richard Francis Weymouth

Products Designed for Today's Children and Youth

And Jesus Healed Them All (confession book and
  CD gift package)
Baby Praise Board Book
Baby Praise Christmas Board Book
Noah's Ark Coloring Book
The Best of *Shout!* Adventure Comics
The *Shout!* Giant Flip Coloring Book
The *Shout!* Joke Book
The *Shout!* Super-Activity Book
Wichita Slim's Campfire Stories

World Offices of
Kenneth Copeland Ministries

For more information about KCM and a free
catalog, please write the office nearest you:

Kenneth Copeland Ministries
Fort Worth, Texas 76192-0001

Kenneth Copeland
Locked Bag 2600
Mansfield Delivery Centre
QUEENSLAND 4122
AUSTRALIA

Kenneth Copeland
Post Office Box 15
BATH
BA1 3XN
U.K.

Kenneth Copeland
Private Bag X 909
FONTAINEBLEAU
2032
REPUBLIC OF
SOUTH AFRICA

Kenneth Copeland
Post Office Box 378
Surrey, B.C.
V3T 5B6
CANADA

Kenneth Copeland Ministries
Post Office Box 84
L'VIV 79000
UKRAINE

We're Here for You!

Believer's Voice of Victory Television Broadcast

Join Kenneth and Gloria Copeland and the *Believer's Voice of Victory* broadcasts Monday through Friday and on Sunday each week, and learn how faith in God's Word can take your life from ordinary to extraordinary. This teaching from God's Word is designed to get you where you want to be—*on top!*

You can catch the *Believer's Voice of Victory* broadcast on your local, cable or satellite channels.

*Check your local listings for times and stations in your area.

Believer's Voice of Victory Magazine

Enjoy inspired teaching and encouragement from Kenneth and Gloria Copeland and guest ministers each month in the *Believer's Voice of Victory* magazine. Also included are real-life testimonies of God's miraculous power and divine intervention into the lives of people just like you!

It's more than just a magazine—it's a ministry.

Shout! The Voice of Victory for Kids

Shout!...The dynamic magazine just for kids is a Bible-charged, action-packed, quarterly magazine available FREE to kids everywhere! Featuring Wichita Slim and *Commander Kellie and the Superkids*_{SM}, *Shout!* is filled with colorful adventure comics, challenging games and puzzles, exciting short stories, solve-it-yourself mysteries and much more!!

Stand up, sign up and get ready to *Shout!*

To receive a FREE subscription to *Believer's Voice of Victory,* or to give a child you know a FREE subscription to *Shout!*, write to:

Kenneth Copeland Ministries
Fort Worth, Texas 76192-0001

Or call: 1-800-600-7395   (7 a.m.-5 p.m. CT)
Or visit our Web site at: **www.kcm.org**

If you are writing from outside the U.S., please contact the KCM office nearest you. Addresses for all Kenneth Copeland Ministries offices are listed on the previous pages.